Suzette
and the Puppy

A Story About Mary Cassatt

Joan Sweeney • Illustrated by Jennifer Heyd Wharton

BARRON'S

No matter how cold the weather in Paris, Suzette's nursemaid

Marie believed in daily outings in the fresh air.

That's how they first happened to meet Nipper. One wintry day, they were hurrying through the park, all bundled up, when they saw a tall lady coming from the other direction. As they passed, a shaggy little head popped out of the lady's blue velvet muff.

Suzette squealed with delight. It was the tiniest dog she had ever seen! The lady stopped and bent low so the little girl and her nanny could see the dog better.

"This is my new puppy, Nipper," she told them. "Isn't he sweet?" The little dog cocked his head to the side, raised one ear, and glanced up at the sound of his name.

Suzette was captivated. But Marie was telling her to say au revoir. As she reluctantly followed her nursemaid home, Suzette hoped Nipper would be in the park the next day.

Yet it was some months before they saw Nipper again. One afternoon after a spring shower, Suzette and Marie noticed a strange sight on the path.

A doll-sized yellow slicker seemed to be marching through the mist. They soon realized it was the puppy, dressed for the rain.

"All he needs is an umbrella!" said Marie, laughing.

They watched him splash through a puddle in his miniature boots, tugging on the leash his tall mistress held.

"Isn't Nipper's rain costume splendid?" she asked. They giggled at the words.

As the days warmed and nature burst into bloom, Suzette and Marie frequently met the other nursemaids and their small charges in the park. To everyone's delight, a handsome policeman was often there, too.

The children shrieked with laughter at puppet shows in the shade of the trees, and played hide-and-seek among the daffodils. They loved to sail their toy boats on the circular pond.

But their greatest pleasure came from seeing the tall lady and her little dog. Nipper would bark wildly when a gust of wind sent the sails flying. Then he would dash along shore with the tall lady racing behind.

"Alors!" the policeman would say, laughing. "We should arrest the little fellow for disturbing the peace!"

Each noon when the church bells rang, Marie spread a coverlet on the grass. Then she and Suzette shared a basket of croissants, cheese, and fruit.

A fter that Suzette was expected to nap.

But the day Nipper created the greatest excitement, there was no napping for anyone.

It all began when someone tossed a rubber ball into the pond. Nipper's ears stood at attention as he watched it splash among the boats and bob to the surface.

"Nipper! S'il vous plait!" the tall lady scolded, gripping his leash. His tiny tail twirled.

Then it happened. Nipper broke away, took a headlong leap, and dove into the pond after the ball.

"Nipper!" the lady shrieked. "Mon Dieu! Good gracious!" In her excitement, she mixed her French with her English.

Nipper appeared to sink to the bottom. All around there were cries of alarm.

"Save him, monsieur!" Suzette sobbed to the policeman. "He will surely drown."

Marie held her back. "Nonsense! The pup can swim like a fish," she told her. "Every dog can."

It was true. Nipper had surfaced and was calmly paddling toward the ball. But the policeman had already stripped off his cape and boots.

"Fear not," he shouted. "I will rescue him."

At that, he held his nose and jumped into the pond with a huge splash, only to hit the bottom with a thud, for the water was only knee-deep.

By then Nipper was heading toward shore. The policeman sloshed after him, pushing fish and toy boats aside. He had nearly caught up with the swimming pup when he stumbled backward, flapping his arms wildly, and plunged into the pond with the greatest splash of all.

Catastrophe! Disaster! All those nearby were hit by the deluge.

Meanwhile, Nipper scrambled onto the bank. He shook
himself from head to toe, thoroughly soaking everyone again.

"Nipper, you little devil!" sputtered the tall lady. "If I didn't
love you so, I *would* have you arrested for disturbing the peace!"

That afternoon, everyone used Marie's coverlet for a towel.

With a smile, the nursemaid told the tall lady, "Too bad he wasn't wearing his rain costume."

The lady agreed. "Too bad we weren't *all* wearing rain costumes."

The bedraggled policeman was wringing out his socks. "Merci beaucoup, Nipper!" he said. "I haven't had such a refreshing bath in years!"

The tall lady scooped up her little dog tenderly. Wet as they both were, they exchanged even wetter kisses.

That evening at supper, Suzette, now crisp and fresh, was eager to tell about the day's events. But her parents had far more exciting news to report. The following day, they told her, a dear friend of Uncle Edgar's was coming to start painting her portrait.

Suzette blushed with pleasure, ever so surprised.

But not nearly as surprised as she was the next morning. Because who should arrive at the door, carrying a sketchbook and pastels?

None other than the tall lady from the park! And with her was Nipper.

"I've hoped to do your portrait ever since I first saw you last winter," the artist explained.

"I'm truly honored," Suzette declared, just as Mama and Papa had told her to say.

Then she begged, "But please! Can Nipper be in the picture, too?"

That was the beginning of what became a
beautiful painting. It's called *Little Girl in a
Blue Armchair* and now hangs in a famous
American museum.

Perhaps you wonder why the little girl and
the tiny dog look so bored. Clearly they would
much rather be playing in the park.

Little Girl in a Blue Armchair (1878) is the beautiful Mary Cassatt painting featuring Suzette and Nipper. In this study they really do seem to wish for another adventure in the park rather than posing for a portrait. *Collection of Mr. and Mrs. Paul Mellon, ©2000 Board of Trustees, National Gallery of Art, Washington.*

The tall lady in the story is modeled after the celebrated American artist, Mary Cassatt. Among the best of the American Impressionists, she is considered the outstanding woman painter of the nineteenth century. Her best-known works portray affluent women in social settings and mothers with small children.

Born to a wealthy Pennsylvania family in 1844, she attended the Academy of Fine Arts in Philadelphia. She went to Europe to continue her studies by copying Old Masters in the major museums there, and settled in Paris in 1872.

Her work attracted the admiration of the French artist Edgar Degas, who invited her to join the Impressionist group. *Little Girl in a Blue Armchair* (Suzette in the story) was the daughter of friends of Degas. The Griffon terrier (Nipper in the story) was a gift from Degas to Cassatt. And Degas even helped to paint the background of this picture. As in the story, the real Nipper had a fashionable wardrobe, including a raincoat.

Cassatt urged her American friends to acquire Impressionist art and was influential in promoting its popularity in the United States. She died in France in 1926.